ABOUT MAGIC READERS

ABDO continues its commitment to quality books with the nonfiction Magic Readers series. This series includes three levels of books to help students progress to being independent readers while learning factual information. Different levels are intended to reflect the stages of reading in the early grades, helping to select the best level for each individual student.

Level 1: Books with short sentences and familiar words or patterns to share with children who are beginning to understand how letters and sounds go together.

Level 2: Books with longer words and sentences and more complex language patterns with less repetition for progressing readers who are practicing common words and letter sounds.

Level 3: Books with more developed language and vocabulary for transitional readers who are using strategies to figure out unknown words and are ready to learn information more independently.

These nonfiction readers are aligned with the Common Core State Standards progression of literacy, following the sequence of skills and increasing the difficulty of language while engaging the curious minds of young children. These books also reflect the increasing importance of reading informational material in the early grades. They encourage children to read for fun and to learn!

Hannah E. Tolles, MA Reading Specialist

www.abdopublishing.com

Published by Magic Wagon, a division of ABDO, PO Box 398166, Minneapolis, Minnesota 55439. Copyright © 2015 by Abdo Consulting Group, Inc. International copyrights reserved in all countries. No part of this book may be reproduced in any form without written permission from the publisher. Magic Readers™ is a trademark and logo of Magic Wagon.

Printed in the United States of America, North Mankato, Minnesota.
062014
092014

THIS BOOK CONTAINS RECYCLED MATERIALS

Cover Photo: Thinkstock
Interior Photos: iStockphoto, Shutterstock, Thinkstock

Written and edited by Rochelle Baltzer, Heidi M. D. Elston, Megan M. Gunderson, and Bridget O'Brien
Illustrated by Candice Keimig
Designed by Candice Keimig and Jillian O'Brien

Library of Congress Cataloging-in-Publication Data

O'Brien, Bridget, 1991- author.
  Deer in the woods / written and edited by Bridget O'Brien [and three others] ; designed and illustrated by Candice Keimig.
     pages cm. -- (Magic readers. Level 3)
  Audience: Ages 5-8.
  ISBN 978-1-62402-065-0
  1. White-tailed deer--Juvenile literature. I. Keimig, Candice, illustrator. II. Title.
  QL737.U55O273 2015
  599.65'2--dc23
                     2014005841

Magic Readers

level 3

Deer
in the Woods

By Bridget O'Brien
Illustrated photos by Candice Keimig

Magic Readers
An Imprint of Magic Wagon
www.abdopublishing.com

White-tailed deer live in North America, Central America, and South America.

They live in the woods. They also live in fields and meadows.

Deer live near their favorite foods. They also need fresh water.

Sometimes deer live near people.
They like to snack on gardens!

Deer share their home with wild turkeys, squirrels, and many kinds of birds and snakes.

Deer are like elk, moose, and reindeer.

Elk

Moose

Reindeer

White-tailed deer are very common.

Two other kinds are mule deer and black-tailed deer.

Mule Deer

Black-Tailed Deer

White-tailed deer have good senses of sight and hearing.

Their sense of smell is even more important.

A deer uses its senses to stay safe from predators.

It looks around and sniffs the air. It moves its ears to listen carefully.

If a deer senses danger, it may stand very still.

When danger is near, a deer flips up its tail. This warns other deer.

Deer can also run away fast!

A fawn can easily follow the white tail to safety.

Wolves, mountain lions, coyotes, bears, bobcats, and jaguars eat deer.

Wolves

Mountain Lions

Coyotes

Bears

Bobcats

Jaguars

People also hunt deer.

To find deer, people look for tracks. Bigger tracks lead to bigger deer!

A hoofprint is shaped like two teardrops.

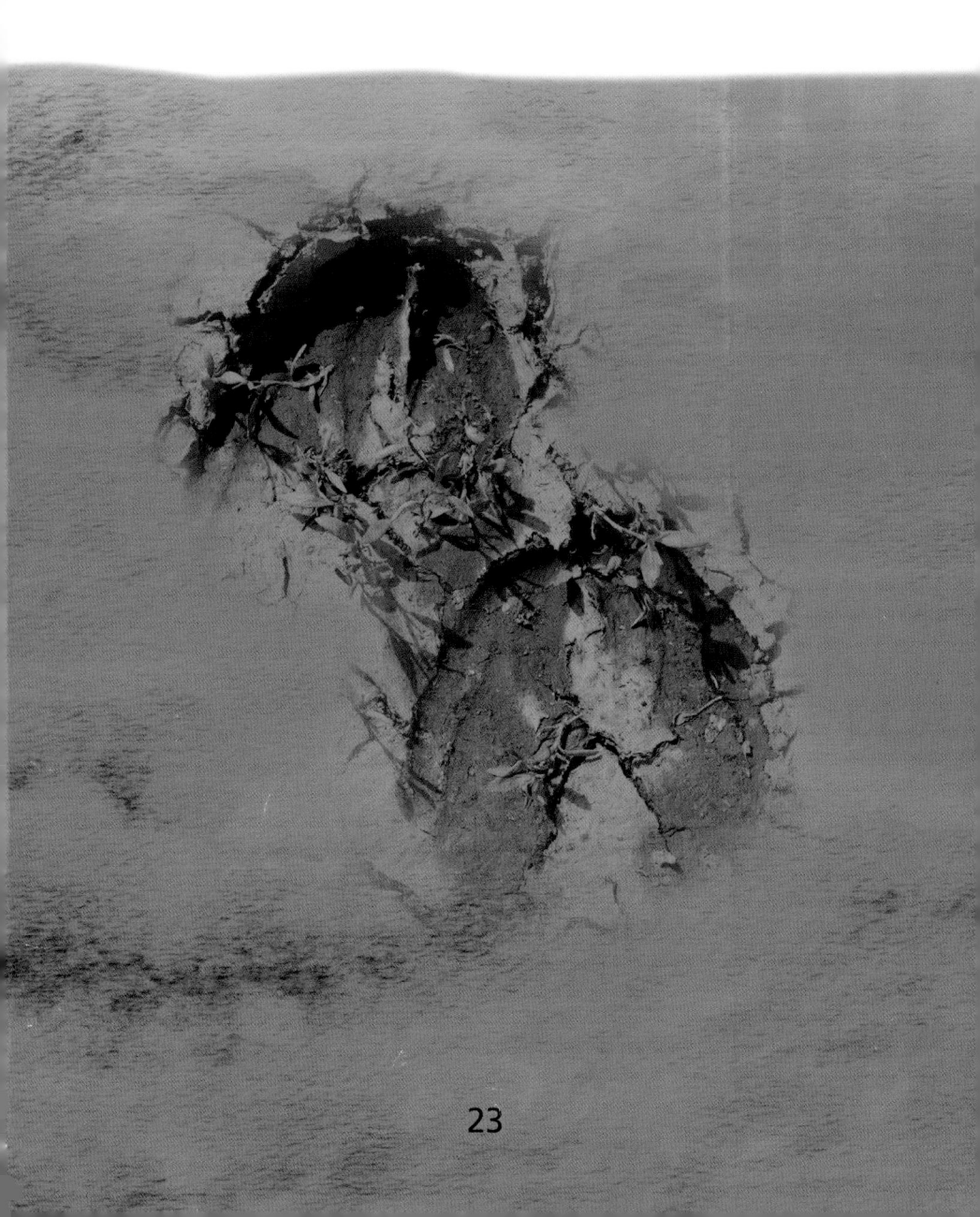

People see deer in parks, zoos, and even backyards!

DISCARD